POWER AGAINST BEWITCHMENT

Insightful Revelation about Bewitchment with Effective Prayers to Conquer Bewitchment at All Levels

By

Augustine Ayodeji Origbo

ISBN: 9798333582263

Unless otherwise indicated, all scriptural references are from the Authorized King James Version.

TABLE OF CONTENT

Dedication

Acknowledgments.

Chapter One: What does it mean to be bewitched?

Chapter Two: Types or forms of bewitchment

Chapter Three: Signs of a bewitched Life, Family, Community or Nations

Chapter Four: Causes of bewitchment

Chapter Five: Instruments or tools used by demonic agents for bewitchment

Chapter Six: Steps to dealing with bewitchment

Chapter Seven: Effective Prayer against the power of Bewitchment

ABOUT THE AUTHOR

□

Dedication

I dedicate this book to all those who are going through one form of difficulties or the other as a result of demonic bewitchment and manipulations ; I therefore trust there expectation will be met through the instrumentality of this book.

□

Acknowledgments.

Special acknowledgment to the almighty God who gave the revelations and the wisdom to write this book.

Have respect unto the covenant: for the dark places of the earth are full of the habitations of cruelty. O let not the oppressed return ashamed: let the poor and needy praise thy name. Psalm 74:20-21

Chapter one

WHAT DOES IT MEAN TO BE BEWITCHED?

To be bewitched simply mean:

1. To deliberately cause an alteration into a life, a family, a thing, an organisation, a system, so as to make them malfunction or suffers terrible experience or very negative consequences;

2. It is to demonically programmed a person out of God"s divine purpose to satanic purpose.

3. It is to change the original objective of a life into a very wrong and unproductive objectives

4. It is to divert a person, a family, a thing, or a system from good intention into a devilish intention.

5. It is to engage demonic mechanism to compel an individual, group of individual, family, organisation,

community, nation to do or carry out the intentions or the will of the compeller.

6. It is to wickedly change the destiny of a person, family, community, system or organisation, nation i.e to make them unproductive and unsuccessful.

7. It is to be forced to be doing the biddings of your enemies

8. It is to be enslave by destiny devourers and glory amputators

9. It is to be at the mercy of a demonic agents or demonic strongman/strongwoman

10. It is using a demonic mechanism to cause confusions and chaos where peace of mind is expected or supposed to reign.

11. It is to influence a person or a family, or group of community to do bad or negative things that will bring negative consequences or the judgement of God upon them.

12. It is to tamper with a progressive life, business, family, marriage, nation,

resources to make them unprogressive and unresourceful.

13. It is to be influence against your will.

O foolish Galatians, who hath bewitched you, that ye should not obey the truth, before whose eyes Jesus Christ hath been evidently set forth, crucified among you? Galatians 3: 1

Chapter two

TYPES OR FORMS OF BEWITCHMENT

For a better understanding of what bewitchment means, I want to highlight in this chapter the various forms or types of bewitchment around as this will go a long way to help you to deal with them using the divinely inspired prayer solutions in this book.

1. **INDIVIDUAL OR PERSONAL BEWITCHMENT**: this form of bewitchment happens when an individual life and destiny is targeted for manipulations and destruction by the evil ones, for example Mr X family spent all their life savings to sponsor Mr X education. As soon as Mr X graduated from the higher institution. Mr X suddenly die in a vehicle accident on his way home to announce his success to his parent. He died unable to fulfil his

destiny on earth because of demonic bewitchment by evil programmer.

2. **FAMILY BEWITCHMENT**: this happens when an entire family is targeted for demonic manipulations or destruction. Some demonic agents like witches, wizard and marine spirit can because of the forseen bright and glowing future of a family decide to throw demonic charms or arrows on the family to prevent such bright and glowing future from happening. If you noticed a family where almost all the family members have been imprisoned for one crime or the other, such family are suffering from bewitchment. In a family where the father died from drug addiction and the children follow suit that family is suffering from the arrow of bewitchment. There are also family, where the father is a drunkard, the mother is a drunkard and the children also follow the same pattern of lifestyles; bewitchment is also in operation in such family. My prayers Is that as you read this book, every form of bewitchment

operational in your family shall be destroy, in the mighty name of Jesus christ.

3. COMMUNAL OR TRIBAL BEWITCHMENT: this happens when a whole tribe or community is programmed to do the biddings of satanic agents, so that the glory of God for the people in such community will not be able to manifest. For instance there are community where days are dedicated to worship satan, demons and deities. Such community and it inhabitants has be bewitched and they may find it very difficult to develop and make progress. In a bewitched community, fornication, banditry, drunkenness, evil addictions, lack of development, jealousy and regular quarrels or fights among themselves are the norms of that community. It is in a bewitched community that people are demonically prevented from building new houses, as inhabitant are regularly attacks with charms to prevent any progress of the people and the land. Bewitched communities are only known with their red rusted and outdated roofing because no one have build a new house for years. It is also common to note that, Unplanned road, unkept streets, lot of mad or insane people on the street corners are attributes of a bewitched community. Most young men in a bewitched community will rather gather under the trees or in a park in the community corners to smoke, take drugs, get drunk or gossips rather than seeking to pursue personal development that may bring personal and life fulfilment.

4. **NATIONAL BEWTCHMENT**: this happens when the whole inhabitant or citizen of a nation is programmed into the patterns of lifestyles that does not depict God divine plans for them, thereby making almost everyone to do the wrong things that will jeopardize growth, national development and stop divine virtues from manifesting in the life of the inhabitants. This are some of the signs you may noticed in a bewitched nation:

a. National day of demonic festival, idol or deities worship and ritual pratices

b. Extreem banditry

c. Long time war and terroism

d. A very high rate of divorce

e. High level of occultism and secret societies

f. Lot of homeless children and adult .

g. Lot of street beggars expecially children

h. False religion with very large followers

i. High rate of drug consumptions and addictions

j. High rate of prostitution

k. Political and social instability

l. Very corrupt society

m. Inhabitant or citizen hate their country and most likely will prefer to go abroad

n. Very arrogant and corrupt leadership at the helms of affair.

o. Sabotage to development and national growth by selfish individuals without the fear of God. Etc.

5. BUSINESS OR ORGANISATIONAL BEWITCHMENT: this happen when an organisation, church, ministry or a business is to fail rather than progress. This may sound strange to many, but this is possible. Many company or businesses have bankrupted today not because the managements do not know how to run the company well, but because the businesses has been manipulated by demonic forces to fail and close down. A pastor once share a testimony of how God deliver his church from the manipulation of demonic bewitchment. He said despite every efforts made the church simply refuse to grow, until he engages in spiritual warfare that opened his eyes to see the activities of the power of darkness bewitching the church. He exercise his divine authority and commanded those forces to disappear, and they obey him. If he had not seen the revelation that lead to the action he took; the church will have remain stagnated. Few year ago I also had a revelation of a church that simply refuse to grow simply because some marine agents all dressed in white cloths and with chalks marks all over their body will not allow the church to progress. When a business or an organisation or a company is bewitched, such bewitched company or business will began to experience regular breaking down of equipment, losses, regular errors, embezzlements, sudden death of employers or key employees, strange fire accident and business image problem. If such business owner do not pray hard against arrow of bewitchment such business owner may not come out of debt forever. Pls note that all mismanagement are programmed arrow of bewitchment.

Chapter three

Signs of a bewitched Life, Family, Community or Nations

What are the problems associated with a bewitched life, family, community or nation, in other words what are the signs that indicate that a person, a family or nation is suffering from bewitchment? let us going examine some signs that indicate that a person life, family, community or nations has been bewitched.

1. **Consistence failing at the edge of success or breakthrough**: This happens when you have work very hard and you are about to experience success and breakthrough, suddenly everything just turn against you and you fail and lost out, that is bewitchment in operation.

2. Bewitchment happens when someone who is living abroad and earning a very good livelihood is demonically manipulated with a charm

or fetish by satanic agents to forget everything he or she has abroad and return home to His or her village to become a peasant farmer or even a street beggars

3. When you are always taking wrong decisions or wrong directions that brings you problems and lost. That is a sign of bewitchment..

4. **Business, Church or Organization failure**: When a business, a church or an organization refuses to grow after the best effort, strategies or policies are employed, then; the forces or agents of bewitchment are the one blocking the growth of such establishment. I shared in the previous chapter how a pastor overcome the power of bewitchment against the Church he was pastoring. Despite every efforts made, his church simply refuse to grow, until he engages in spiritual warfare that opened his eyes to see the activities of the power of darkness bewitching the church. He exercise his divine authority and commanded those forces to disappear, and they obey him. If

he had not seen the revelation that lead to the action he took; the church will have remain stagnated. When a church, an organization or a company is bewitched, such bewitched company or business will assuredly began to experience problems like breaking down of equipment, losses, financial difficulties and misappropriation of funds, regular errors, embezzlements, sudden death of employers or key employees, strange fire accident and business image problem. If such business owner do not pray hard against arrow of bewitchment such business owner may not come out of debt forever.

5. When a person who Is beautiful, intelligent and fit for marriage is unable to get a husband or get married after several marriage proposals, arrow of bewitchment may be in operation.

6. Joblessness: having the best of certificate but still unable to get a profitable job after years of graduation, please you need to pray against the arrow of bewitchment.

7. **When a person experiences** seasoner madness, that is when a person will usually go mad or insane at a particular time or period yearly, bewitchment is in operation.

8. **Sudden madness:** When a successful and happily married man or woman suddenly become mad or insane, arrow of bewitchment is in operation.

9. **Sudden blindness:** when someone who is well to do, suddenly become blind and could not live happily again, bewitchment is in operation.

10. When a man suddenly develop strange affections for his daughter and began to have sex with her or when a woman began to have sexual relationship with her own son, the arrow of bewitchment is in operational in their life.

11. **Living abroad but Living in Misery:** Some people's decision to travel abroad for greener pastures did not originate from God at all. They were simply programmed by the arrow of bewitchment to quit their land of nativity

where God may have destined them to become great and be celebrated. These people, because of their desperation, which in most cases is programmed by witches, might have sold all their belongings back home in order to fund their relocation abroad. By the time they eventually get abroad and discover that their aspiration of picking money on the streets in a foreign land is not met, frustration and misery will set in. They won't be courageous enough to return home because of the fear of humiliation and the fear of starting afresh. If such person does not pray very hard, he may not be able to understand that his destiny has been tampered with by Witchraft powers who want him to amount to nothing in life and so moved him out of his place of blessings.

12. All paedophiles, homosexuals, prostitutes and transvestites are under the demonic

13. **When a person choose scamming and swindling as profesion or carrier such person destiny and life has been**

bewitched. Naturally such person may think swindling or robbing others of their wealth is a good way to get rich or make easy money, not knowing that swindling or robbery gives demonic agents access to waste their time and life and also prepare destructions for their yet unborn Children. You need to pray for deliverance so that you can discover your destined purpose and work hard to fulfill them, so that your future generation will not face any regrets. Pls note that anyone who is fraudulent or corrupt today is actually preparing destruction and a frustrated future for their children, this is because the bible afirm that God visit the sins of the father on the children or offspring if they do not repent.

14. Livig a promiscuous lifestyle is a sign of bewitchment: That is when you are happily married but secretly having sexual relationship with other women or men that you are not married with.

15. Rising and Falling In life and business: This happens when a person experiences a remarkable level of progress and after a while encounters a gruesome level of failure. Such person need to pray against the arrow of bewitchment.

16 Evil inherited pattern of Insanity: when an evil patterns of insanity is operational in a lineage; taking for instance, if you notice or have been told that someone in your lineage must become insane, every 10 or 15years, such family must have been bewitched by satanic agents.

17. Once very rich and well to do but now very poor, miserable and homeless: When a person who is well to do in life suddenly lost everything he possessed to afflictions or theft to suddenly becomes a beggar, such person has been bewitched

18. Spirit of procrastination: this happens when a person who is inspired to start a profitable and beneficial projects that can positively transform lifes and generations decides to keep postponing the projects until they are never actualises or accomplished during their life time.

Satanic agents may have bewitched them to keep postponing the projects, until they are old and weak to bring the projects into realisation.

19. Odd in the Family: This happen if among your siblings you are the only one who is poor, miserable, unemployed and unproductive. Despite been the eldest you are finding things very difficult in life, such that you sometime have to literarily beg to feed, then you will need to seriously pray against the arrow of bewitchment.

20. Programmed Error: If anytime you are employed or awarded a contract, you notice that you will always make one mistake that will often lead to the termination of your appointment or contracts. This is simply arrow of bewitchment in operation.

21. Spirit of wastage: This happens when as soon as a person is renumerated or paid salary, strange problem will just come up to take the money from the person or individual hand.

22. **Confusion:** When you are confuse about life and such confusion almost pushed you to kill yourself or to taking dangerous substances, arrow of bewitchment has been programmed against you.;

23. **Barriers to life progress:** This happens when after you have put so much effort into a project and you are about to be rewarded, suddenly an obstacles that will just frustrate your effort will come and make your projected will be rejected or frustrated.

24. **Evil Circle of inherited Hardship and poverty:** Suffering similar hardship to that of your living or dead ancestral parents. Taking for instance, If your father is a very poor bus driver, and you, despite your university education ends up a poor taxi driver that can not avoid to feed well, this are signs of a bewitched life.

25. **Disappointments:** disappointment can be program into a life through the arrow of bewitchment for instance, when

several beneficial promises and appointments made to you end up in successive disappointment,

26. Begging for everything: When a person is not ashame to beg for anything to make himself or herself comfortable; some people can beg for food, beg for money, beg for cloths, beg for shoes, beg for shelters e.t.c such person is under serious demonic bewitchment.

27. Sudden pregnancy without knowing who the father is a sign of a bewitched life

28. Stagnantion and the spirit of backwardness: This happens when after putting so much efforts into your projects, business or ministry, instead of enjoying progresss, you are experiencing stagnation and sometimes consistent regression or backwardness.

29. Sexual harassment in the dream: If you have seen yourself once or twice been molested sexually in the dream while asleep in the night or during the day, You need to pray very had against the spirit of bewitchment. Spirit spouse might have been introduced into you life to bewitch you and frustrate your life and destiny.

30. **Addictions:** When a very brilliant and intelligent boy, girl, man or woman suddenly becomes addicted to destructive habit like taking prohibited Drugs (i.e cocaine), Drunkeness, theft, betting, Masturbation, Pornography, etc such person have been afflicted with the arrow of bewitchment.

31. **Barrenness:** Some barrenness today irrespective of the medical expertise employed may never turn to fruitfulness, this is because a person can be bewitched from becoming pregnant through demonic charms by agent of darkness. Until spiritual solution is engaged, certain act of barrenness may never turn to fruitfulness.

32. **Fornicating without remorse:** Living and having sexual intercourse with a man or woman without marriage is a sign of bewitchment. Every sexual

relationship without the seal of marriage on it bring demonic covenant into the life of parties in such unholy sexual relationship and every demonic covenants will automatic leads to demonic manipulation or bewitchment

33. Children bewitchment: When a very brilliant boy or girl in school suddenly become dull and develop hatred for school or learning. Arrow of bewitchment may have been fired against that child. You will need to pray fervently to destroy such demonic bewitchment and free that child from such arrow.

34. Spirit of hatred: When you are been hated everywhere you go or in whatever you do, you need to pray against the arrow of bewitchment

35. Total disobedience to parent: When your once obedient and very understanding children suddenly develop total disobedient to you, you need to start praying against the arrow of bewitchment.

36. Evil patterns of Bad luck: If you noticed that everybody seems to be suffering from similar problem of failure, divorce, poverty or disappointments in your family, then you need to pray against the yokes of bewitchment of evil patterns of badluck operational in your life and family

Other signs of a bewitched life, family, community and Nation are:

37. Seasoner sickness: that is having to fall sick at a particular period of the year.

38. When a man suddenly becomes a slave to his spouse, simply living at the mercy of his wife; confuse, and not knowing how to direct his life , home and family affairs, he has been bewitched

39. Chronic hardship

40. Constant Rejections

41. Strange anger or agitation

42. When a person has serious hatred for profitable knowledge

43. Desire to commit suicide

44. Been Constantly depressed

45. Spirit of lust
46. Intelligent but low life perfomance
47. Regular bad dream
48. Life without a purpose
49. When been pursue regularly in the dream
50. Very dull brain
51. Working hard but having little or nothing to show for it
52. Marriage to your enemy
53. Consistence Divorce
54. Murder and shedding of innocent bloods
55. Marriage to the wrong woman
56. Marraiage to the wrong man
57. Regular communal conflict are sign of a bewitched community
58. Banditry, conflicts and war ravage communities or nation implies that such places are under demonic bewitchment

59. Very low level of development in a nation or community can also be traceable to demonic bewitchment.

60. If you are presently in your early twenties, thirties or going to forty and you have not discover the reason why you are born. In other words, you are already an adult and you do not have a purpose for living and you are not even bothered about discovering your purpose in life so as to fulfil your destiny on earth, then you have been bewitched, you need to pray the prayers in this book so as to be free from the cage of ignorance that destiny destroyers may have put you in.

Chapter Four

Causes of Bewitchment

What are the Factors that can open a person life to bewitchment

1. Shedding of innocent blood by ones ancestors: If your ancestor had Shed the blood of an innocent person in the past, and the sin have not yet been confessed to God so as to obtain total forgiveness and cleansing, you are likely going to be attack by demonic agents of bewitchment who will want your own life as a replacement for the innocent blood shed by your ancestors. Until you ask for forgiveness from God and pray hard to break the yoke of your ancestors error in your life, agent of bewitchment will continue to molest you and your offsprings life and destiny.

2. Ancestral Worship of idols or deities: if your ancestor have worship demonic being like, heros, deities in the past, your life is already exposed to the

activities of demonic demoters, who will not rest until they see that you are not celebrated in your generation.

3. Robbery, cheating or swindling: if your ancestors have lived a life of robbery, cheating or swindling, that is, to swindle other persons of their properties or wealth, your own life may be in danger of the activities of demonic destroyers who will not rest until you are bewitched and becomes miserable. The only way to escape the consequences of this kind of sin is to repent of your ancestral sin and break away totally through prayers from their benefits.

4. Polygamous family history: if you are born from a polygamous family , you also need to seriously pray against the arrow of bewitchment

5. Living in a haunted or a bewitched house: Another thing that can open a person life to bewitchment or to demonic agents of bewitchment is to ignorantly buy or rent a bewitched or haunted house for personal use. If you are presently living in a house and you noticed that

your landlord or other persons usually come there to make sacrifice or ritual to a deity, then that house and the inhabitant is already bewitched. The fact is that the governor of that house is the spirit behind the deity or idol that they regularly come to worship in that compound. All houses where people worship or make sacrifices to deities or idols are demons embassy. Living is such house will make life miserable for the inhabitants; imaging a person living with demons in the same compound, that person should expect a baptism of bewitchment

6. If you are not yet born again, in other words, if you have not yet submitted your life to the lordship of our lord and saviour Jesus Christ, then you are expose to the activities of agents of darkness who can just attack or bewitch you at will. Actually the sins of humanity first parent (Adam and Eve) brought demonic dominion and bewitchment upon the human race. But the price for the sin were paid for by our Lord Jesus christ on the cross at calvary. Men can now have their security or protection in

the blood of Jesus Christ against demonic attacks and all form of bewitchment, if the confess him as their Lord and saviour.

7. Immoral acts: living an immoral life itself is a sign of bewitchment. dwelling or perpetually living in sin like adultery, fornication, masturbation, porns addiction, theft, money swindling(known as 419), usage of charms and fetish objects, strange anger, picking regular quarrels and fighting etc opens the doors of those doing them to demonic attacks and subsequently bewitchment.

Chapter five

Instruments or tools used by demonic agents for bewitchment

Here are some tools or means through which demonic agents bewitched their victims:

1. **Evil utterances:** This are words spoken under the influence of demonic power or spirit against any things living or non living i.e a person, a family, business, or house , objects etc to make such things obey of do the biddings of the demonic agents making such utterances;

2. **Demonic Spells:** Spells are simply demonic elements used by demonic agents to change the destiny of their victims to what they like or want. In other words, spells can include seen or unseen demonic substances that can be applied to the body, food, sexual organs, tea, beer or drink, perfumes, etc. for the purpose of bewitching or evil manipulation.

3. **Demonic waters:** Please note that not all pure water or bottled water that

are available on the market today are truly pure, some are produced and distributed by demonic agents to bewitched people or manipulate human. That is why you need the spirit of discernment and be very prayerful. Praying on all the waters you buy for drinking will go a long way to help your life against the activities of Witchcraft agents. Many because of thirst will just buy packaged or pure water and start drinking without praying or pleading the blood of Jesus on it, from there they will just fall victims to destroyers of destinies.

4. **Fetish:** fetish objects as an instrument of bewitchment can be buried in the ground on the compound of a business, organisation and family house to cause disaster to life and business. Fetish can also be programmed to manipulate a person or system to become malfunction or fonction abnormal.

5. **Demonic or haunted house:** Some houses are worse to live in than the graveyard. Some people deliberately build houses to bewitch their tenants and

rob them of their glory. In a haunted house, nothing good will ever happen in the life of the inhabitant. Backwardness, loss of life, strange diseases, business failures, demonic attacks by strange beings at night and sexual harassment in dreams are the usual experiences of those who live in bewitched houses. If the occupant of a demonic or bewitched house does not pray, calamity upon calamity may become his usual experience.

6. Food in the dream: One of the easiest way through which demonic agents bewitched their victims is through food been feed to them In the dream. When an enemies sees that they can not destroy a person in the physical world they usually will pass through the spirit relm to feed them with demonic and abominable food, so that they can control or manipulate them to do their biddens in the real or physical world. So, if you are the type that eat regularly in the dream, you need to pray the prayers in this book against demonic bewitchment targeted at your life.

7. **Dirty money:** Dirty money is the proceeds of demonic or ungodly activities that can be used to manipulate the destiny of the innocent person who is rewarded with it. Such money includes stolen money, ritual money, corrupt money, money stolen or swindled by very corrupt politicians etc. Dirty money is used by demonic agents as an instrument of paralysis and bewitchment on anyone who uses it for their own gratification. If a ritualist gives you money, it is your destiny that will be targeted for destruction in exchange for the reward of the money given to you. Please note that all dirty money or unlawfully acquired money are instrument of bewitchment, in other words, all ungodly or unlawfully acquired money or wealth is an enchanted money or wealth. Spending it will make you and your descendants a cursed person.

8. **Demonic street hawker:** Some of the groundnuts and bean cakes (known as akara in the Yoruba language) bought from street vendors are not ordinary food. They have been bewitched by demonic agents. Many have eaten them and has been initiated into the demonic world without knowing, while others have been robbed of their intended greatness. If you are the type of person who usually patronises roadside food hawkers, you need to pray. Although not all roadside food vendors are Satanic agents, you must still be very careful and pray very well over whatever you buy to eat.

9. **Demonic properties**: properties like clothes , shoes, phones, handkerchief, framed artworks etc, are also been used by satanic agent to bewitched people, When demonic items or properties like this are brought or introduced into a house, calamities will suddenly befalls the user and their family members. If the users are not prayerful they may not know where the source of their problems

come from. I once slept in the house of a friend years ago. While asleep, suddenly I had a very short revelation, in that revelation, i notice that a personality came down from the image on the framed artwork they put on the wall of their house. They probably may have bought or given the artwork as a gift without knowing the spiritual implications of hanging such item in their house. Unknowingly, they have brought a bewitched item home

10. Demonically programed sex: another mean through which a person can be bewitched is through sexual intercourse with a human agents of darkness. An agent of darkness (female/male) can be instructed or programmed to have sexual relationship with an ignorant person. From there their victim semens can be take and transfer into the demonic world for evil manipulations or bewitchment. Such a victim who has had such sexual intercourse with the demonic agent will just be miserable on earth suffering from failure and hardships

11. **Demonicaly inspired music:** regular dancing or listening to demonic music can lead to the transfer of evil virtues and subsequently a demonic transfer into demonic world and every demonic transfer into the spirit world will lead to demonic initiation, evill manipulation or bewitchment

12. **Sex in the dream:** demonic agents who may be finding it difficult to access a person in the physical world may access the person life through sex in the dream to pollute or transfer evil deposits into their victim life to cause them to be miserable here in the real world

13. **Spiritual husband and wife**: the spirit husband and spirit wife are agents of bewitchment. The spirit husband/wife are evil spirit that transform into familiar, likeable or close relative image or faces to appear to people in the dream so as to have sexual intercourse with them so that their destiny can be

bewitched and or control from the spirit world

14. **Demonic roadside food sellers:** There are roadside food seller who still engage the use of fetish or charms on their food in order to increase sale and have more customer. Through such manipulation of their food and their place of selling, many who eat such food without proper prayer have eating calamities and problems. A brother once share a revelation he had sometime again. In the revelation, he saw a young child who bought something from a roadside food seller to eat, in that same revelation he saw how the child grew up and become a masturbator. That is bewitchment in action.

Other instrument of bewitchment includes

15. Demonic barber or hairdressers who are of the habits of selling their customer hair at a price to witchdoctors or ritualist who will further use such hair for ritual money or self empowerment.

One reason you need to carefully and prayerfully choose the barber or hairstylist that touch your head.

16. Generation curses
17. Incatations
18. Demonic perfumes
19. Jinx
20. Curses
21. Program sexual intercourse in the dream
22. Unholy sexual relationships
23. Poisons
24. Poisonned fruits

Chapter Six

Steps to dealing with bewitchment

What are the things you need to do in order to be able to overcome the power of bewitchment

1. **Give your life to Jesus Christ:** The true and effective power to overcome bewitchment and other demonic attacks and manipulations on earth today can only be gotten from God. And to access this power of God, you need to accept Jesus Christ as your Lord and Saviour. Christ death on the cross of calvary was for the purpose of putting an end to the suffering and calamities brought upon man by the sins of humanity first parent Adam and Eve. Because God is the master yoke breaker and master burden lifter. He has all power in His care and specialises in breaking all kinds of yokes including the yokes of bewitchments. God is and will be willing to destroy the power of bewitchment in your life and family if only you will accept Jesus Christ

into your life today and confess him as the saviour of your soul from sins. Matthew 11:28–30 says,

Come unto me, all ye that labour and are heavy laden, and I will give you rest. Take my yoke upon you, and learn of me; for I am meek and lowly in heart: and ye shall find rest unto your souls. For my yoke is easy, and my burden is light.

Just as the scriptures afirm, God is the only one who can remove the burdens of bewitchment that Satanic agents have placed on you, your family, your ancestor and your community. However, you need to come to Him acknowledging that He is your God and that He has paid a great price for your redemption by dying for the sins that open the access to demonic attacks into your life on the cross at Calvary. Galatians 3:13–14 says,

Christ hath redeemed us from the curse of the law, being made a curse for us: for it is written, Cursed is every one that hangeth on a tree: That the blessing of Abraham might come on the Gentiles through Jesus Christ; that we might receive the promise of the Spirit through faith.

You need to accept Him as your Saviour and Lord in order to receive the promise of the spirit through faith by saying the following prayers:

Lord Jesus Christ, I acknowledge that I am a sinner who needs your mercy. I believe you died for my sins on the cross at Calvary. Forgive me all my sins. Come into my life and give me the eternal life that will guarantee me victory over bewitchment and satanic attacks. Thank you Lord Jesus Christ for saving me.

If you have said those words of prayer, then you are now a child of God. Your identity has change. You now has the authority to manifest as a child of God and obtain victory over bewitchment and other satanic attacks by demonic agents. You can now stand with authority in the place of prayer to ask God for mercy and help.

But as many as received him, to them gave he power to become the sons of God, even to them that believe on his name John 1:12

2. **Withdraw from ungodly lifestyles:** withdraw totally from ungodly life, fornication, adultery, cheating, lying etc. Also usage of charms, or possession of fetish objects should be totally abandone so that the enemies will not use such things as as another access into your life

3. **Make sure you give your tithes and offerings to God minister or to your local Church,** as this will help you against the activities of evil devourers and also make you eligible to pray against them

"Even from the days of your fathers ye are gone away from mine ordinances, and have not kept them. Return unto me, and I will return unto you, saith the LORD of hosts. But ye said, Wherein shall we return? Will a man rob God? Yet ye have robbed me. But ye say, Wherein have we robbed thee? IN TITHES AND

OFFERINGS (emphasis mine). Ye are cursed with a curse: for ye have robbed me, even this whole nation. Bring ye all the tithes in the store house, that there may be meat in mine house, and prove me now herewith, saith the LORD of hosts, if I will not open you the windows of heaven, and pour you out a blessing, that there shall not be room enough to receive it. And I will rebuke the devourer for your sakes, and he shall not destroy the fruit of your ground; neither shall your vine cast her fruit before the time in the field, saith the Lord of hosts. And all nations shall call you blessed: for ye shall be a delightsome land, saith the LORD of hosts." (Malachi 3:7–12)

Pls note that those who program bewitchment into people life are agents of satan and all agents of satan and their master lucifer are devourer. So in other to position your life and family for effective prayers and victory, you need to be a giver of tithes and offerings to God.

4. Be ready to fast and pray with the prayers in this book.

Chapter Seven

Effective Prayer against the power of Bewitchment

Sing praises and worship to God for 15-30 minutes

Bible reading: Deuteronomy 23

READ THE FOLLOWING BIBLE CONFESSIONS

Matthew 11:28-30

"Come unto me, all ye that labour and are heavy laden, and I will give you rest. Take my yoke upon you, and learn of me; for I am meek and lowly in heart: and ye shall find rest unto your souls. For my yoke is easy, and my burden is light".

2 Chronicles 7:14-16

"If my people, which are called by my name, shall humble themselves, and pray, and seek my face, and turn from their wicked ways; then will I hear from heaven, and will forgive their sin, and will heal their land. Now mine eyes shall be open, and mine ears attend unto the prayer that is made in this place. For now have I chosen and sanctified this house, that my name may be there for ever: and mine eyes and mine heart shall be there perpetually"

Colossians 3:13–15

"And you, being dead in your sins and the uncircumcision of your flesh, hath he quickened together with him, having forgiven you all trespasses; blotting out the handwriting of ordinances that was against us, which was contrary to us, and took it out of the way, nailing it to his cross; and having spoiled principalities and powers, he made a shew of them openly, triumphing over them in it."

Isaiah 54:17

"No weapon that is formed against thee shall prosper; and every tongue that shall rise against thee in judgment thou shall condemn. This is the heritage of the servants of the LORD, and their righteousness is of me, saith the LORD."

Mark 11:23–24

"For verily I say unto you, that whosoever shall say unto this mountain, Be thou removed, and be thou cast into the sea; and shall not doubt in his heart, but shall believe that those things which he saith shall come to pass; he shall have whatsoever he saith. Therefore I say unto you, What things soever ye desire, when ye pray, believe that ye receive them, and ye shall have them."

Isaiah 53:4–5

"Surely he hath borne our griefs, and carried our sorrows: yet we did esteem him stricken, smitten of God, and afflicted. But he was wounded for our transgression, he was bruised for our iniquity: the chastisement of our peace was upon him; and with his stripes we are healed."

Numbers 23:23

Surely there is no enchantment against Jacob, neither is there any divination against Israel: according to this time it shall be said of Jacob and of Israel, What hath God wrought!

Psalm 18:6–7

"I call upon the LORD in distress: the LORD answered me, and set me in a large place. The LORD is on my side. I will not fear what man can do unto me"

Joel 2:25

"And I will restore to you the years that the locust hath eaten, the cankerworm, and the caterpillar, and the palmerworm, my great army which I sent among you."()

Pray these prayers with all your heart.

1. Almighty God I thank you for your goodness and loving kindness towards me and my family, in Jesus Christ's name.

2. Eternal Father I thank you for showing me your love through the death of your Son on the cross at Calvary, in Jesus Christ's name.

3. I exalt you heavenly father for you alone are worthy of exaltation.

4. Thank you O God for making provisions for my deliverance and salvation from all bondage in your word, in Jesus Christ's name.

5. I honour you almighty Father for all honour, power, wisdom, strength, blessing, glory and riches belong to you, in Jesus Christ's name.

6. I come before you eternal Father and confess all my sins and my ancestral sins before you today in Jesus' name. (Confess your sins right from childhood and those of your ancestors, as many as you can remember, before the Lord.)

7. I renounce my involvement in....... (Mention every evil association that you may have been involved with in the past, including while you were still very young) in the name of Jesus Christ.

8. I confess before the Lord almighty that I am separated from occult practice, idolatry, adultery, robbery, whore mongering, etc. in Jesus Christ's name.

9. I nullify any consequences of my belonging to any evil associations in the past in the mighty name of Jesus Christ.

10. I nullify every curse that I have issued against any person, family, land or community consciously or unconsciously by the power in the blood of Jesus, in the name of Jesus.

11. By faith I dip myself in the pool of the blood of Jesus Christ, in the name of Jesus Christ.

12. By faith I drink the blood of jesus Christ for the healing of my Spirit, Soul and Body, in the mighty name of jesus christ

13. Through the blood of Jesus Christ, I purge myself from any demonic deposit that I may have benefited from by virtue of my past involvement in any evil gathering or association, in the name of Jesus Christ.

Destroying or breaking evil covenant that can open doors to demonic bewitchment

14. I break and seperate myself totally from every conscious or unconscious covenant with Satan, in the mighty name of Jesus Christ.

15. I break and seperate myself totally from every conscious and unconscious covenant with the Queen of heaven, in the name of Jesus Christ.

16. I break and seperate myself totally from every conscious and unconscious covenant with the serpentine spirit in the name of Jesus Christ.

17. I break and seperate myself totally from every conscious and unconscious covenant with the Queen of the Coast, in the name of Jesus Christ.

18. I break and seperate myself totally from every conscious and unconscious covenant with the marine spirit and its kingdom, in the name of Jesus Christ.

19. I cancel all evil covenants made on my behalf with any idol by my ancestors by the eternal power in the blood of Jesus Christ, in the name of Jesus Christ.

20. I break and seperate myself totally from every conscious and unconscious covenant with any witch or wizard, in the name of Jesus Christ.

21. I break and seperate myself totally from every conscious and unconscious covenant with the idol of my father's and mother's house in the name of Jesus Christ.

22. I break and seperate myself totally from every conscious and unconscious covenant with the evil idols of my community, in the name of Jesus Christ.

23. I break and seperate myself totally from every conscious and unconscious covenant with the evil idols of my place of birth, in the name of Jesus Christ.

24. I separate myself from every idol and related spirit by the power in the blood of Jesus Christ.

Destroying the foundation or bewitchments

25. By the power in the blood of jesus christ I separate myself from the power of

collective captivity of my father's house, in the mighty name of Jesus Christ

26. By the power in the blood of jesus christ, I separate myself from the power of collective captivity of my mother's house, in the mighty name of Jesus Christ

27. Foundation of bewitchment in my family scatter by fire, in the mighty name of Jesus Christ.

28. You tree of bewitchment in my lineage, dry up by fire, in the mighty name of Jesus Christ.

29. Every demonic chain tying my down to any idol, break by the fire of God and by the power in the blood of Jesus Christ, in the mighty name of Jesus Christ.

30. Ancestral debt collector seeking for my head, perish, in the mighty name of Jesus Christ

31. Destiny waster that has chosen me and my family for destruction, in the mighty name of Jesus Christ, I command all the destruction that you have wished

for me and my family to come upon your head in the mighty name of Jesus Christ

32. Power hiding in the dark to throw me arrows of misfortune, slump and die, in the mighty name of Jesus christ

33. Misfortune, misfortune, misfortune, die, in my life today, in the mighty name of Jesus Christ

Break the power of spell and incantations

34. Spells assigned to make me beg in life, backfire to the senders in the mighty name of Jesus Christ

35. Spell and incantations that turn beauty to ashes assigned against my life, backfire to senders, in the mighty name of Jesus Christ.

36. Spells working against my business scatter by God divine fire, in the mighty name of Jesus Christ

37. Any object projected into the elements against my happiness, loose your power and scatter by fire, in the mighty name of Jesus Chrits

38. Demonic object buried in the ground to make me a failure in life, catch fire and burn to ashes, in the mighty name of Jesus Christ

39. Spells programmed into to the sun against my happiness be neutralised today, in the mighty name of Jesus Christ.

40. You enchanter, enchanting me and member of my family, catch fire and be disgraced in the mighty name of Jesus Christ

41. Yoke of Spell of addiction to drugs operational in …… life (please put the name of the person you know is addicted to drugs in the gap) break into pieces today, in the mighty name of Jesus Christ

42. Spells working against my destiny, scatter by God divine fire, in the mighty name of Jesus Christ

43. Demonic spell working against my business, loose your power over my business and scatter by fire, in the mighty name of Jesus Christ.

44. Satanic odour place upon my business to drive away my customer, be wise out by the power in the blood of Jesus Christ

45. Evil odour place upon my life by the past evil deeds of my ancestors, that is now driving away destiny helpers from me, expire today and be destroy by the power in the blood of Jesus Christ, in the mighty name of Jesus Christ.

46. Satanic perfums working havoc in my life, lose your power Iver my life today, in the mighty name of Jesus Christ.

47. You evil pattern of bewitchment operational in my fathers life, that want to began it evil activities in my own life, die today, in the mighty name of Jesus Christ.

48. Family plagues dictating the direction of my life and destine, be quenched today, in the mighty name of Jesus Christ.

49. Spells programmed against my financial life, scatter by God divine fire, in the mighty name of Jesus Christ

50. Spells and enchantments programmed against my siblings(mention your siblings name), scatter in the mighty name of Jesus Christ

51. Spell casted on me from my mothers womb, loose you power over my life and catch fire, in the mighty name of Jesus Christ

52. Evil cries from my community/village demons or idols speaking failure and backwardness into my life and family, be eternally silenced by the blood of Jesus Christ, in the name of Jesus Christ.

53. You national curses, inherited curses, self-acquired curses, listen to me, because I am now a member of the family of Jesus Christ, pack your load, leave my life and return no more, by the power in the blood of Jesus Christ, in the might name of Jesus Christ.

54. You ancestral curse executor assigned against my life and my family, receive divine paralysis, in the name of Jesus Christ.

55. You demonic curse executors that pursued my ancestors and are now pursuing me, in the name of Jesus Christ, the name that is above all names, I command thunder and fire from God to demolish you and all the instruments you are using against me, in the mighty name of Jesus Christ.

56. Demonic curse executors appointed over my life, family, and business, perish, in the name of Jesus Christ.

57. Evil curse executors appointed over the indigenes of my land of nativity, that are now after my life and family, receive divine earthquake and be eternally destroyed, in the name of Jesus Christ.

58. Causes that is saying that I will never reach the top of the ladder of success in life, die today, in my life in the mighty name of Jesus Christ.

Prayer against monitoring spirit

59. Evil eyes monitoring the progress of my life, become blind from this minutes, in the mighty name of Jesus Christ.

60. Monitoring gargets of the enemies of my soul, malfunction right now in the mighty name of Jesus Christ

61. Witches and wizards that are gathered against my life progress, receive divine fire from God and be burnt beyond recognition, in the mighty name of Jesus christ

62. Marine powers that are gathered against my life progress, receive divine fire from God and be burnt beyond recognition, in the mighty name of Jesus christ

63. You evil spirit around following me and my family member all around, perish today, in the mighty name of Jesus Christ.

64. Every familiar spirit assigned by satan to monitor my life into destruction, i destroy you in the mighty name of Jesus Christ.

65. Satanic memory bank where events of my life are been documented to be use against me, scatter into pieces and catch fire, in the mighty name of Jesus Christ.

66. Camera of darkness around my vicinity assigned to monitor me and my family member, scatter by fire, in the mighty name of Jesus Christ

67. Evil power that has been following me since I was born, get away from me today by the power in the blood of Jesus Christ

68. Power assigned to monitor me to failure, die, in the mighty name of Jesus Christ.

Sending back evil arrows

69. Arrows of failure assigned against my life and family backfire to senders in the mighty name of Jesus Christ

70. Arrow of backwardness programmed against my business, jump ou of my business right now and backfire to the senders in the mighty name of Jesus Christ.

71. Arrow of bad lucks assigned against my life and destiny backfire right now to the senders in the mighty name of Jesus Christ

72. Programmed arrows of madness jump out of the life of…… (please mention the name of anyone that is suffering from madness or insanity that you know) in the mighty name of Jesus Christ

73. Arrrow of madness programmed into my lineage that is now trying to attack my life, hear the word of the Lord, I am not your candidate, scatter into pieces and catch fire, in the mighty name of Jesus Christ

74. Any thing buried on the ground to manipulate my life and that of my family member, be exhumed and backfire to your sender, in the mighty name of Jesus Christ

75. Arrows of darkness killing my business, come ot of my business and backfire to the sender, in the mighty name of Jesus Christ

76. Arrow of rising and falling operational in my life,die today, in the mighty name of Jesus Christ

77. Arrow of joblessness operational in my life,die today, in the mighty name of Jesus Christ

78. Arrow of rejections fired against my head, jump out now, and backfire to the sender, in the mighty name of Jesus Christ

79. Arrow of masturbation programmed against my life to render me useless and unproductive, jump out of my life and catch fire, in the mighty name of Jesus Christ

80. Arrow of pornography addiction programmed into my foundation jump out of my foundation and perish in the mighty name of Jesus Christ

81. Arrows of addiction to drugs and dangerous substances programmed into my life, hear the word of the LORD, loose your power over my life today and perish, in the mighty name of Jesus Christ.

82. My destiny jump out of the grave of self destruction, in the mighty name of Jesus Christ.

83. Demon aligned to execute bewitchment in my destiny, drink the blood of Jesus Christ and become paralysed in the mighty name of Jesus Christ.

84. I close, by the power in the blood of Jesus Christ every doors in my life that is open to satanic invasion, in the mighty name of Jesus Christ.

85. I scatter by fire every coven of darkness where demonic decision are been made against my happiness in the mighty name of Jesus.

86. Powers siting inside the ocean to bewitch me and my household, drink the blood of Jesus Christ and be Judged by God divine fire in the mighty name of Jesus Christ.

87. Judgement of fire from God, fall upon every power persecuting me because of my great future, in the mighty name of Jesus Christ.

88. I shall no die, but live to fulfill my destiny, in the mighty name of Jesus.

89. I cancel by the blood of Jesus Christ every sickness and infirmity programmed into my life to stop me from fulfilling my destine goals in life, in the mighty name of Jesus

90. Sickness and infirmity I am not your candidate, loose your grip over my life and be uprooted out from your root in the mighty name of Jesus.

91. Infirmity targeted at my life to make me lost faith in my God, die today, in the mighty name of Jesus Christ .

92. Satanic bird programmed to monitor my success catch fire and burn to ashes in the mighty name of Jesus Christ.

93. Animal of darkness targeting my next blessings and breakthrough, die, in the mighty name of Jesus Christ.

94. Anyone inside my family throwing evil arrows of at me, receive the judgement of God and be disgraced in the mighty name of Jesus Christ.

95. Every agents of darkness pretending to be my friend in order to

arm me, receive the judgement of God and be disgraced in the mighty name of Jesus Christ.

96. By the power in the blood of Jesus Christ, I break myself loose from the power of charms, spell, incantation, in the mighty name of Jesus Christ.

97. Power assigned to stop me anytime I am about to make progress in life, drink the blood of Jesus Christ today and be eternally paralysed, in the mighty name of Jesus Christ.

98. Anything in my life that is attracting demonic attacks to me, catch fire, in the mighty name of Jesus Christ.

99. I destroy by the blood of Jesus Christ every agreements made by my ancestors with dark powers to stop my progress, in the mighty name of Jesus Christ.

100. I nullify the evil effects of food eating in the dream to frustrate my life, in the mighty name of Jesus Christ Marine.

101. Demonic food programmed into my life through the dream to paralyse my life and destiny, catch fire and burn to ashes, in the mighty name of Jesus Christ.

102. I cancel the evil effects poisonous foods, drinks, water and fruits taking in my dreams by the power in the blood of Jesus Christ, in the mighty name of Jesus Christ.

103. Agent of darkness assigned to polite my destiny through sex in the dream, drink the blood of Jesus Christ and receive the judgement of fire from God,in the mighty name of Jesus.

104. I come out of every coven of darkness where satanic deliberation and invocation is been made upon my head unaware by the blood of Jesus Christ.

105. Satanic image, pictures, statutes representing me in the coven of darkness, scatter by fire and burn to ashes, in the mighty name of Jesus Christ.

106. Any power using my picture to afflict me on an evil altars, receive divine

judgement and be destroy, in the mighty name of jesus christ.

107. Power using my pictures to bewitch my life, received God judgement of fire and be burn to ashes, in the mighty name of Jesus christ;

108. Power using my pictures to bewitch me, received God judgement of fire and be burn to ashes, in the mighty name of Jesus christ;

109. Family witchcraft altars sending misfortune into my life and destiny, catch fire and burn to ashes in the mighty name of Jesus Christ.

110. Poison of darkness working in my organ to influence my life progress, expire and die today, in the mighty name of Jesus Christ.

111. Battle of barrenness waging war against my life, end today by the power in the blood of Jesus Christ, in the mighty name of Jesus Christ.

112. Battles of lack and want waging war against my life and ministry, end

today by the power in the blood of Jesus Christ, in the mighty name of Jesus Christ.

113. Battles raging against my life that I do not have the power to conquer, Oh! God arrises judge them today by fire, in the mighty name of Jesus Christ.

114. Problems assigned to manifest monthly in my life and family, expire and die today, in the mighty name of Jesus Christ.

115. Problems assigned to manifest yearly in my life and family, expire and die today, in the mighty name of Jesus Christ.

116. Seasonal insanity programmed by the wicked against my lineage, expire today by the power in the blood of Jesus Christ.

117. You demonic personality using the image of my dead family member to attack me in my dream, catch fire and perish, in the mighty name of Jesus Christ

118. Every approval that satan and demons has to torment my life, expire today, in the mighty name of Jesus Christ.

119. Covenant of backwardness operational in my life and family, break, in the mighty name of Jesus Christ.

120. Covenant that has kept my community, nation and continent in captive, that is trying to keep me in captivity, hear the word of the LORD, I am not you candidate, therefore break and loose your hold over my life and family, in the mighty name of Jesus Christ

121. Covenant of affliction from my land of nativity affecting my progress in life, break by God divine fire, in the mighty name of Jesus Christ.

122. Deep rooted covenant blocking my elevation, break by fire in the mighty name of Jesus Christ.

123. Covenant tying me to poverty and misery, beak by God divine fire, in the mighty name of Jesus Christ.

124. I refuse to die in captivity, in the mighty name of Jesus Christ.

125. My injured glory, receive divine healing and manifest according to God's ordained plans, in the name of Jesus.

126. Wherever my glory is been tied down, Rock of Ages release it by fire, in the name of Jesus.

127. Divine oppurtunity that will move me forward, locate me by fire, in the name of Jesus.

128. Divine oppurtunity that will move me forward, locate me right now by fire, in the name of Jesus.

129. I withdraw my blessings from every astral and terrestrial coven constructed by Satan or demonic agents against me and every member of my family, in the mighty name of Jesus Christ'

130. O Lord, position me for divine success and breakthroughs, in the name of Jesus.

131. Power preventing my eyes from discovering my purpose in life, die today, in the name of Jesus.

132. O God, oppen my eyes to see your great plans for my life in the mighty name of Jesus Christ.

133. My family Herod, die in the order of the wicked Herod of old, in the name of Jesus.

134. Chains of darkness and bewitchment hovering over my business, scatter by fire, in the mighty name of Jesus Chrit

135. My blessing kept in the marine kingdom, I recover you by fire, I recover you by thunder, in the name of Jesus.

136. My blessing kept in satanic spiritual bank, I recover you by the power in the blood of Jesus..

137. I declare in the mighty name of Jesus Christ that I am free from all form of bewitchment, in the name of Jesus Christ.

138. Damages done to my life through bewitchment be repaired now by the power in the blood of Jesus Christ, in the name of Jesus christ

139. By faith I bath with the blood of Jesus Christ to free myself from every form of bewitchment, in the mighty name of Jesus Christ

140. I decree and declare in the mighty name of Jesus Christ that all demonic gadgets been use against my progress shall, catch fire and burn to ashes right now, in the mighty name of Jesus Christ

141. Where ever I have used my mouth to say negative things against my life and those negatives things I have said is now affecting my life progress, I cancel those negative words I have said against myself by the power in the blood of Jesus Christ

142. Curses issued against my life because of my past errors, I cancel you today, by the power in the blood of Jesus Christ, in the mighty name of Jesus Christ

143. Curses and evil utterance made against me to make me eat from the

dustbins of life, I cancel you today by the power in the blood of Jesus Christ

144. By faith, I drink the blood of jesus Christ to neutralise the activities of every strange and unseen object operating in my organs, in the mighty name of Jesus Christ

145. By faith I drink the blood of Jesus christ to neutralise every form of addiction operational in my life in the mighty name of Jesus Christ

146. Every strongman or strong woman of darkness that has made up their mind that they will never give until they see my life in failure, Drink the blood of Jesus Christ today, receive also the stone of fire and perish, in the mighty name of Jesus Chrit;

147. I cancel the effects of any evil deposit transfer into my life through sex and kisses in the dream, by the power in the blood of Jesus Christ.

148. Any evil object buried in any house that I have visited or live before, that is now hunting for my success and

progress, be uprooted and scatter by fire, in the mighty name of Jesus Christ.

149. Power appearing in my dream to have sexual intercourse with me, loose your power over my life, by the power in the blood of Jesus Christ, in the mighty name of Jesus Christ

150. Power that has covenanted me to a demonic spirit, die today; in the mighty name of Jesus Christ.

151. I cancel every covenant between me and the spirit husband oor spirit wife, in the mighty name of Jesus Christ.

152. I withdraw all my divine blessings that has been stolen by demonic agents from them by the power in the blood of Jesus Christ

153. From today, I decree and declare that I am totally free and made whole from every effects of bewitchment, by the power in the blood of Jesus Christ, in the mighty name of jesus Christ

154. God's blessings of goodness, favour, fruitfulness and prosperity shall

follow me henceforth from every angle in the mighty name of Jesus Christ.

□

ABOUT THE AUTHOR

AUGUSTINE AYODEJI ORIGBO is the president and founder of The Word of His Grace Evangelical Ministry Int'l., a non-denominational Christian organization whose aim is to reach the unreached and disseminate the undiluted message of our Lord Jesus Christ to the dying world through all the godly and peaceable means available. He is a teacher, evangelist and Holy Ghost-trained global intercessor and counsellor of God's word. He is the author of several Christian and deliverance books, including: Deliverance from the bondage of the spirit husband and wife, Purpose in Life, Recovering Your Lost Glory, a book specially inspired by the Holy Spirit to expose and stop the activities of glory robbers in any life. He is married to Sister Jane and they both work together in the vineyard of the Lord

□

CONTACT ADDRESS:

THE WORD OF HIS GRACE EVANGELICAL MINISTRY INT'L.

OR DELIVERANCE HOUSE MEDIA AND BOOK PUBLISHERS

CONTACT: 002348078166601 or 002348034356069

www.deliverancehouse.org

Benin City

DELIVERANCE HOUSE MEDIA AND BOOKSTORES

Tel: 08034356069, O8078166601

SENEGAL ADDRESS:

Tel: 00221-764958083,

B.p 15577 Dk-Fann

mailto:wgeministry@yahoo.fr, austine_71@hotmail.com

Website

Made in the USA
Columbia, SC
26 December 2024

50619094R00050